FLUTE STUDIES
IN OLD AND MODERN STYLES

VOLUME II

FOR FLUTE

K 02065

CONTENTS

Benoit Berbiguier (1782-1838)
Etude 4

Theobald Böhm (1794-1881)
Allegretto 20
Caprice 8
Caprice 10
Caprice 12
Caprice 16
Risoluto 22
Vivo 36

Fritz Geissler (b. 1921)
Flotenmusik 66

Peter Herrmann (b. 1941)
Caprice 24
Caprice 49
Elegie 22
Fuge 48
Langsam und sehr ausdrucksvoll 38
Scherzo...50

Antoine Hugot (1761-1803) - Johann Georg Wunderlich (1775-1819)
Studie 4

Sigfried Karg-Elert (1877-1933)
Caprice 7
Caprice 12
Caprice 25
Caprice 38
Caprice 55

Sigfried Karg-Elert (continued)
- Caprice 59
- Caprice 63

Günter Kochan (b. 1930)
- Scherzo 6

Ernesto Köhler (1849-1907)
- Etude 26
- Etude 40
- Etude 56
- Etude 60
- Etude 64

Friedrich Kuhlau (1786-1832)
- Divertissement 30
- Divertissement 44

Arnold Matz (b. 1904)
- Adagio 6
- Allegretto 10
- Allegro 17
- Thema mit Variationen 14

Adolf Terschak (1832-1901)
- Etude 52

Unbekannter Meister
- Fantasia 19

Vorschlage fur das Tonleiterstudium 18

Anhang
- Chromatic Study 75
- Vorschlage fur Akkordstudien 72

auch 8va
Originaltonart d-Moll

6

Theobald Böhm (1794 - 1881)

Um ein rundes, klingendes Staccato, besonders in der tiefen Lage zu erreichen, führe man den Atem wie bei einem ausgehaltenen Ton, den man durch erneute Anstöße unterteilt.
Merke: Bleibe mit der Luft am Ton!

Vorstudie

Arbeite diese Etüde vorerst in langsamem Tempo legato, dann portato, non legato und staccato. Die anderen Stärkegrade sind aus dem *piano* zu entwickeln. 8va!

11

Tema con Variationes — Arnold Matz

1) Triller immer Ganzton

12

Caprice Theobald Böhm

Variiere Teile der Studie, z. B. ... Spiele ...

13

Arnold Matz

Anhang

Vorschläge für das Tonleiterstudium

Die angeführten Varianten sind durch alle Tonarten und Oktaven, auf- und abwärts, wie im ersten Beispiel gezeigt ist, zu üben. Verwende verschiedene Artikulationen und Stärkegrade.

Fantasia
Unbekannter Meister des 18. Jahrhunderts

Bemerkung zu Nr. 1
Diese Komposition ist improvisiert im Stile einer Kadenz vorzutragen. Durch langsames Öffnen der Klappen und intensiv ausgeführtes Vibrato wird bei den mit einer Wellenlinie bezeichneten Tönen die Wirkung eines Glissando erreicht, das als reizvolle Verzierung die vorliegende Komposition beleben soll. Als Zählwert sind 8-tel oder 16-tel anzuwenden.

15

Theobald Böhm (1794-1881). op. 37 Nr. 9

Allegretto

Bemerkung zu Nr. 2

Für das Studium der Etüden, die vornehmlich die technischen Fertigkeiten und die Ausdauer des Bläsers steigern sollen, sei auf die im 2. Band der Flötenstudien angegebene Übweise hingewiesen. Ausgehend von der Sicherheit der Ansprache und des Klingens jeden Tones, sind die Studien in Hinsicht auf Dynamik, Artikulation und rhythmische Veränderungen so variabel wie möglich zu gestalten.

18

Caprice

Peter Herrmann

20

Ernesto Köhler (1849-1907), op. 75 Nr. 6

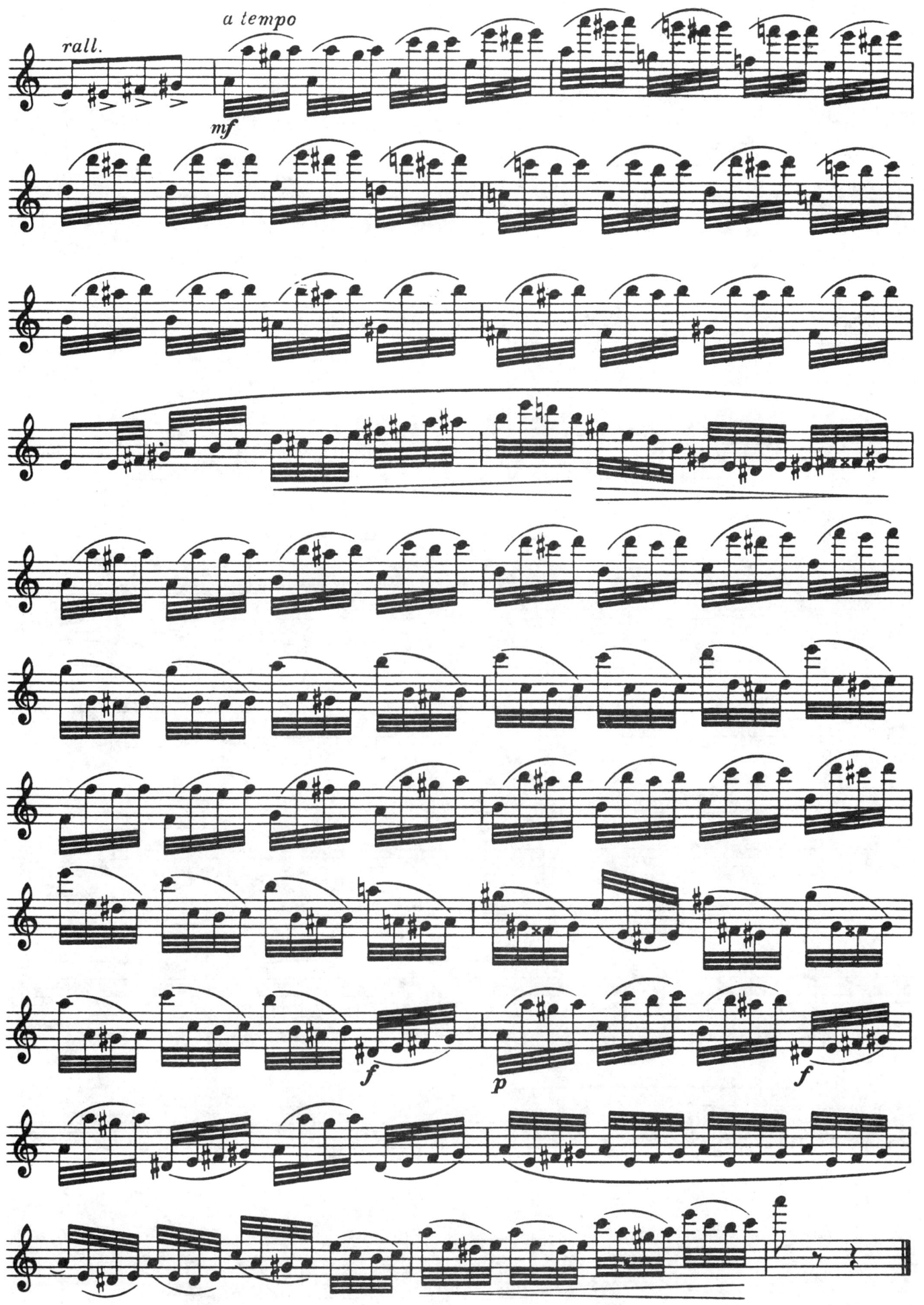

21

Divertissement

Friedrich Kuhlau (1786-1832), op. 68 Nr. 6

22

Theobald Böhm, op. 26 Nr. 14

25

Allegretto mosso[1])

Ernesto Köhler, op. 75 Nr. 26

[1]) Original im punktierten Rhythmus

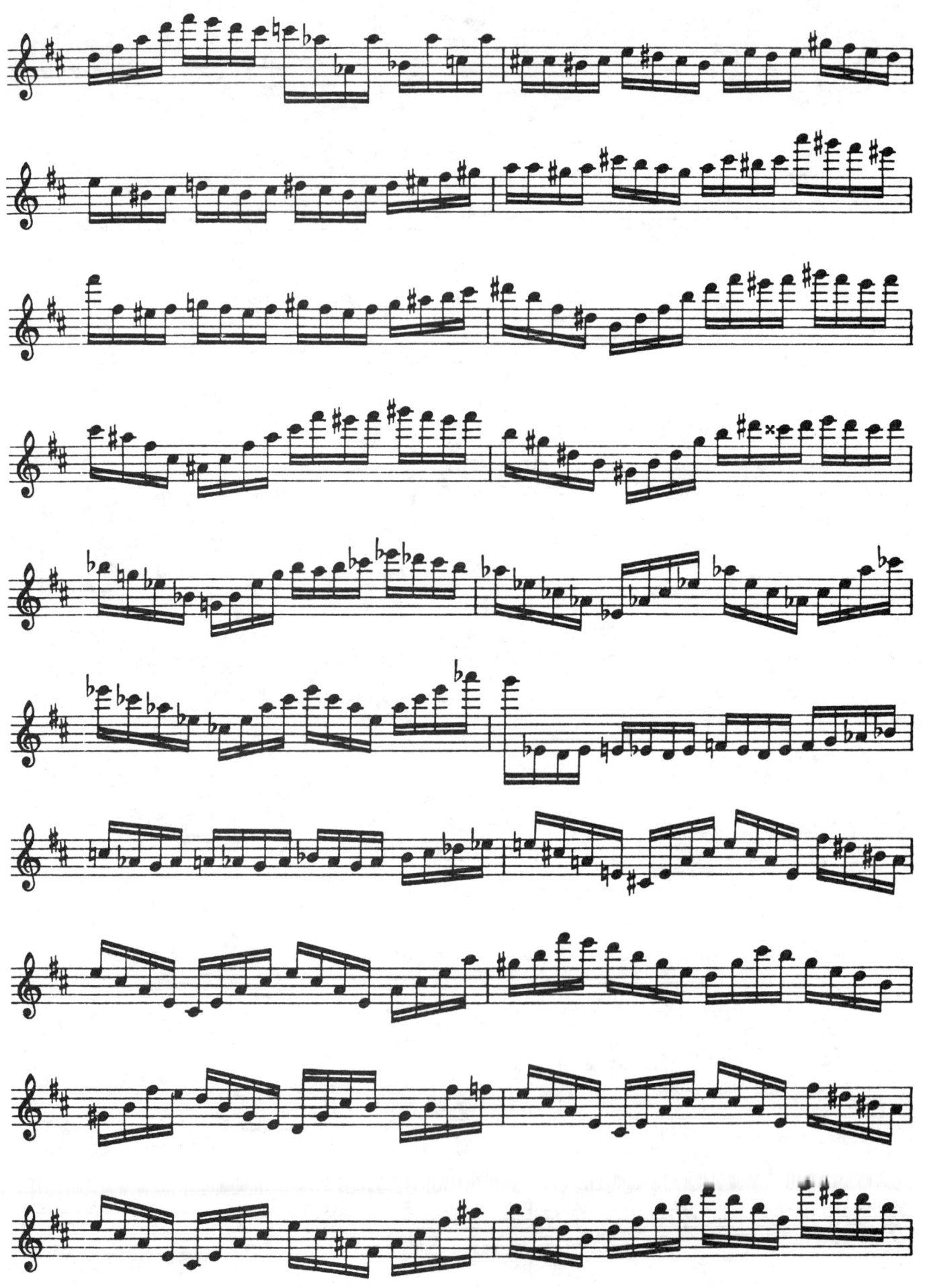

43

26

Divertissement

Friedrich Kuhlau, op. 68 Nr. 5

Original in G-Dur

29

Scherzo

Peter Herrmann

30

nach Adolf Terschak (1832-1901), op. 131

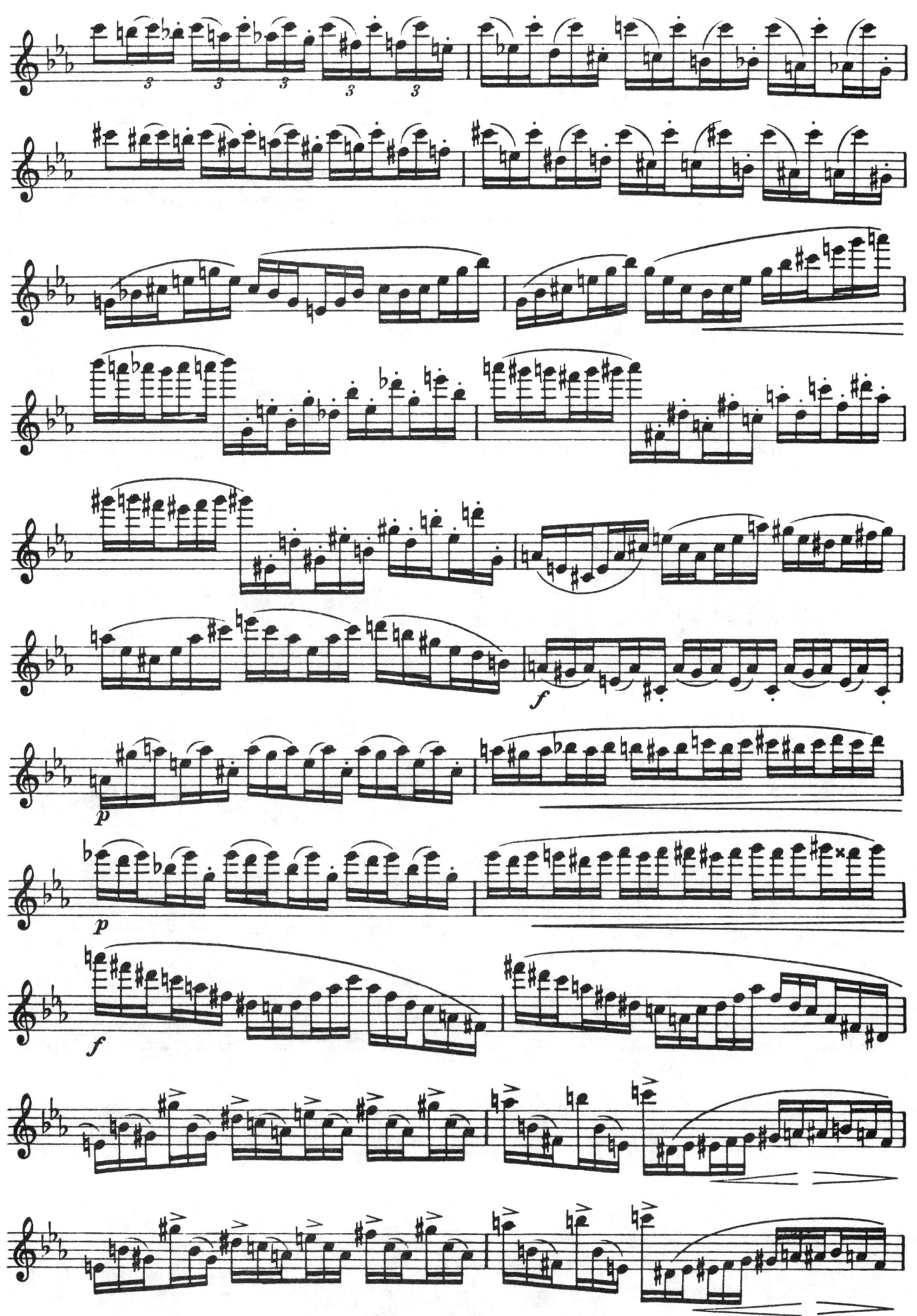

Caprice

Sigfrid Karg-Elert, op. 107 Nr. 25

Un poco vivace e capriccioso (Ziemlich bewegt, kapriziös)

Caprice

Sigfrid Karg-Elert, op. 107 Nr. 22

Agitato ed appassionato (Aufgeregt und leidenschaftlich)

36

Ernesto Köhler, op. 75 Nr. 25

Diese Etüde wurde um einige Takte gekürzt.

37
Flötenmusik

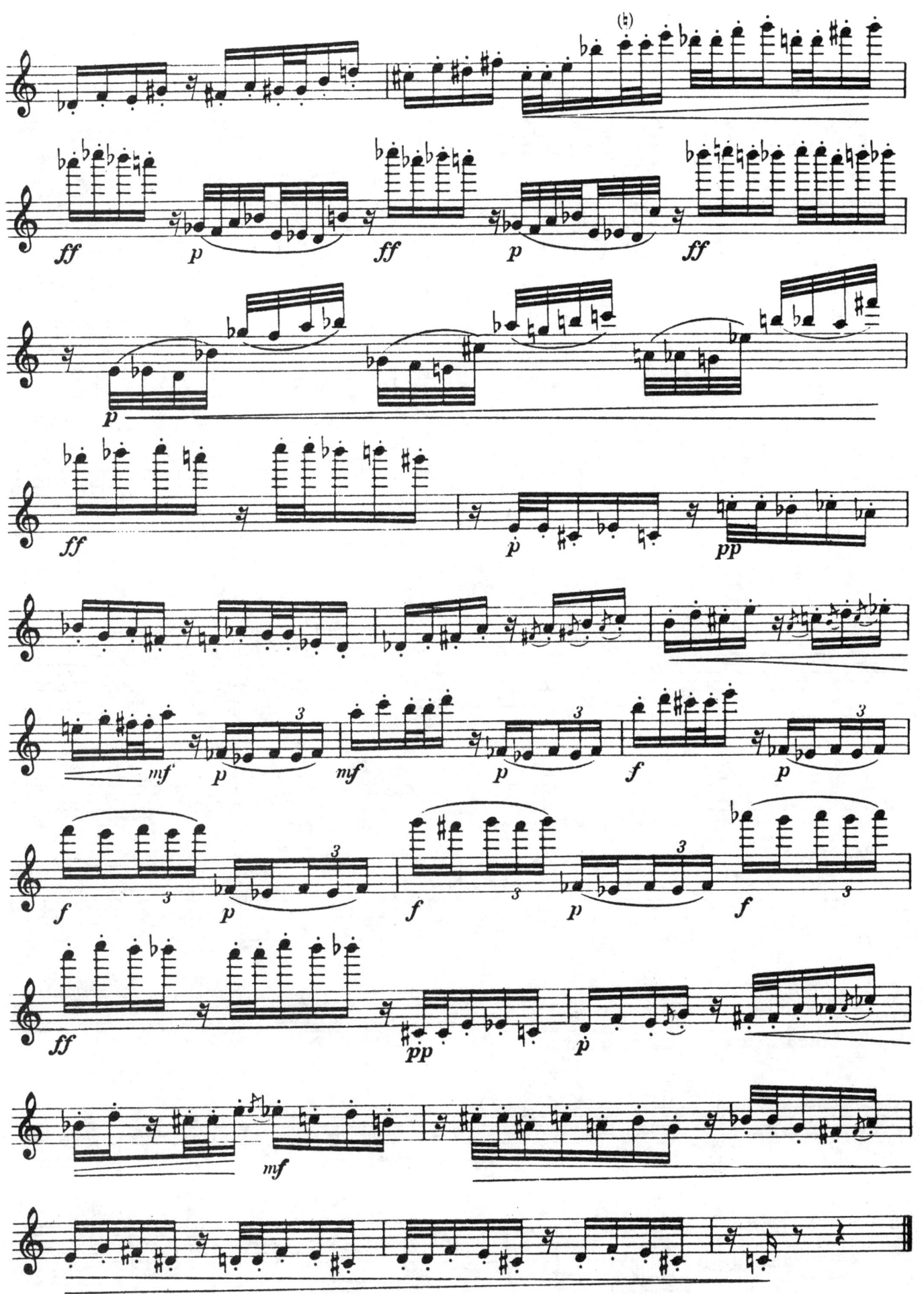

34

Ernesto Köhler, op. 75 Nr. 11

Allegro molto vivace

VI

Anhang

Vorschläge für Akkordstudien, die in allen Tonarten, verschiedenen Artikulationen und in rhythmischen Veränderungen zu üben sind.

*) Die zwischen den einzelnen Figuren eingefügten Zeichen (∥ ∖∖) verkörpern symbolisch die sequenzartige Fortführung der angegebenen Notengruppen.

Chromatische Studien

FLUTE and OBOE

Flute Studies

GARIBOLDI, GIUSEPPE (1833 - 1905)
____ (K04490) 20 Studies, Op, 132
____ (K03431) 30 Easy and Progressive
              Studies — Vol. I
              (Nos. 1-15)
____ (K03432) 30 Easy and Progressive
              Studies — Vol. II
              (Nos. 16-30)

KOEHLER, EMIL (1849 - 1907)
____ (K04493) 30 Virtuoso Etudes,
              Op. 75 — Vol. II
____ (K04494) 30 Virtuoso Etudes,
              Op. 75 — Vol. III
____ (K04496) 20 Easy Melodic Progressive
              Exercises, Op. 93 —
              Vol. I
____ (K04497) 20 Easy Melodic Progressive
              Exercises, Op. 93 —
              Vol. II
____ (K04495) 25 Romantic Etudes, Op. 66

Collections - Flute Studies

FLUTE STUDIES IN OLD AND MODERN STYLES
____ (K04488) Vol. II
____ (K04489) Vol. III

Flute Alone

SCOTT, CYRIL (1879 - ?)
____ (K09727) Ecstatic Shepherd, The

Flute and Piano

BACH, CARL PHILIPP EMANUEL (1714 - 1788)
____ (K03080) Two Sonatas for Flute
              and Piano (G Major and
              E minor)
____ (K03081) Two Sonatas for Flute and Piano
              (A minor and D Major)

BACH, JOHANN SEBASTIAN (1685 - 1750)
____ (K07131) Six Sonatas
              (BWV 1030-1032) Vol. I
____ (K07132) Six Sonatas
              (BWV 1033-1035) Vol. II
____ (K09248) Suite in C minor

DEBUSSY, CLAUDE (1862 - 1918)
____ (K07136) Prelude to "Afternoon
              of a Faun"

ENESCO, GEORGES (1881 - 1955)
____ (K03430) Cantabile and Presto
              for Flute and Piano

FAURÉ, GABRIEL (1845 - 1924)
____ (K03448) Fantasy for Flute
              and Piano, Op. 79
____ (K07135) Sicilienne, Op. 78

GLUCK, CHRISTOPH WILLIBALD von (1714 - 1787)
____ (K09250) Concerto in G Major

GODARD, BENJAMIN (1849 - 1895)
____ (K07139) Allegretto for Flute and
              Piano, Op. 116

HANDEL, GEORGE FRIDERIC (1685 - 1759)
____ (K03520) Seven Sonatas and Largo
              for Flute and Piano —
              Vol. I (Sonatas I - III)
____ (K03521) Seven Sonatas and Largo
              for Flute and Piano —
              Vol. II (Sonatas IV -
              VII and Largo)

LULLY, JEAN-BAPTISTE (1632 - 1687)
____ (K03618) 20 Pieces for Flute (or Violin)
              and Piano

MATTHESON, JOHANN (1681 - 1754)
____ (K03546) 12 Sonatas for Flute and
              Piano — Vol. I
              (Nos. 1-6)

MOSZKOWSKI, MORITZ (1854 - 1925)
____ (K09253) Spanish Dances

MOUQUET, JULES (1867 - 1946)
____ (K07142) La Flute de Pan, Op. 15

MOZART, WOLFGANG AMADEUS (1756 - 1791)
____ (K03723) Flute Concerto No. 1, K. 313
              (G Major) (Orch.)
____ (K03756) Flute Concerto No. 2, K. 314
              (D Major) (Orch.)
____ (K03548) Six Sonatas for Flute and
              Piano — Vol. I (Nos. 1-3;
              K. 10, 11, 12)
____ (K03549) Six Sonatas for Flute and
              Piano — Vol. II (Nos. 4-6;
              K. 13, 14, 15)

QUANTZ, JOHANN (1697 - 1773)
____ (K03810) Flute Concerto (G Major)
              (Orch.)

REINECKE, CARL (1824 - 1910)
____ (K03811) Sonata "Undine," Op. 167 for
              Flute and Piano

SCHUBERT, FRANZ (1797 - 1828)
____ (K09254) Introduction and Variations
              on a Theme "Ihr Blümlein
              Alle," Op. 160

Two Flutes

BACH, WILHELM FRIEDEMANN (1710 - 1784)
____ (K03033) Six Duets for Two Flutes —
              Vol. I (Nos 1-3)
____ (K04731) Two Sonatas

BERBIGUIER, T.B. (1782 - 1838)
____ (K03217) Six Duets for Two Flutes,
              Op. 59

GARIBOLDI, GIUSEPPE (1833 - 1905)
____ (K04734) Six Easy Duets

KUHLAU, DANIEL F. (1786 - 1832)
____ (K03464) Three Duets for Two
              Flutes, Op. 10
____ (K03467) Three Brilliant Duets, Op. 81

Collection - Flute Duets

OLD AND NEW DUETS (MUSIC FROM THE 16th TO 20th CENTURIES)
____ (K04739) Vol. I

Three Flutes

KUHLAU, FRIDRICH (1786 - 1832)
____ (K03133) Three Grand Trios,
              Op. 86 — Vol. I
              (G Major)
____ (K03134) Three Grand Trios,
              Op. 86 — Vol. II
              (D Major)
____ (K03135) Three Grand Trios,
              Op. 86 — Vol. III
              (E Flat Major)

Four Flutes

REICHA, ANTONIN (1770 - 1836)
____ (K03813) Sinfonica for Four
              Flutes, Op. 12

Oboe Studies

BARRET, A.M.R. (1808 - 1879)
____ (K04505) 15 Grand Studies for Oboe
              (with Opt. Bassoon acc.)

MILLE, K.
____ (K04124) 15 Studies

WEIDEMANN, L.
____ (K04125) 45 Etudes for Oboe

Oboe and Piano

HANDEL, GEORGE FRIDERIC (1685 - 1759)
____ (K04513) Two Sonatas

NIELSEN, CARL (1865 - 1931)
____ (K04126) Fantasy Pieces for Oboe, Op. 2

V

WIND INSTRUMENTS

Clarinet Alone

PAGANINI, NICCOLO (1782 - 1840)
____ (K03355)   14 Caprices, Op. 1 and Moto Perpetuo, Op. 11, No. 6

STRAVINSKY, IGOR (1882 - 1971)
____ (K03935)   Three Pieces for Clarinet Solo

Clarinet and Other Instruments

GLAZUNOV, ALEXANDER (1865 - 1936)
____ (K09763)   Ten Duets (Clarinet and Various Instruments)

Clarinet and Piano

(For Clarinet in B-flat, unless otherwise indicated)

BRAHMS, JOHANNES (1833 - 1897)
____ (K03200)   Sonata No. 1 in F minor, Op. 120
____ (K09255)   Sonata No. 2 in E-flat Major, Op. 120

BUSSER, HENRI (1872 - 1973)
____ (K09754)   Un Soir de Mai (au Bois, Op. 4 No. 2 from "A la Villa Medicis")

CLARINET AND PIANO (Cont'd)

DEBUSSY, CLAUDE (1862 - 1918)
____ (K09940)   Petite Piece and Premiere Rhapsodie

ELGAR, EDWARD (1857 - 1934)
____ (K09753)   Canto Popolare

MOZART, WOLFGANG AMADEUS (1756 - 1791)
(K03296)   Adagio
____ (K03776)   Concerto, K. 622 (Orch.)

OFFENBACH, JACQUES (1819 - 1880)
____ (K03297)   La Musette

PIERNE, GABRIEL (1863 - 1937)
____ (K09758)   Piece in G minor

SPOHR, LUDWIG (1784 - 1859)
____ (K03919)   Concerto No. 1, Op. 26 (C minor) (Orch.)
____ (K09747)   Clarinet Concerto No. 3
____ (K09751)   Clarinet Concerto No. 4 (E minor)

WEBER, CARL MARIA von (1786 - 1826)
____ (K03937)   Clarinet Concerto No. 1, Op. 73 (F minor) (Orch.)
____ (K03938)   Clarinet Concerto No. 2, Op. 74 (E-flat Major) (Orch.)
____ (K03936)   Concertino for Clarinet, Op. 26 (E-flat Major) (Orch.)
____ (K03359)   Variations, Op. 33

Two Clarinets

MOZART, WOLFGANG AMADEUS (1756 - 1791)
____ (K04092)   Six Duets for Two Clarinets — Vol. I (Nos. 1-3)

Bassoon and Piano

MOZART, WOLFGANG AMADEUS (1756 - 1791)
____ (K03775)   Bassoon Concerto, K. 191 (Orch.)
____ (K04162)   Two Sonatas for Bassoon and Piano

RIMSKY-KORSAKOV, N. (1844 - 1908)
____ (K04136)   Concert Fantasy, Op. 33

WEBER, CARL MARIA von (1786 - 1826)
____ (K03972)   Bassoon Concerto, Op. 75 (Orch.)

Mixed Woodwind Quintets

(Flute, Oboe, Clarinet, Horn and Bassoon)

KLUGHARDT, AUGUST (1847 - 1902)
____ (K09429)   Quintet, Op. 79

TAFFANEL, PAUL (1844 - 1908)
____ (K09435)   Woodwind Quintet

BRASS INSTRUMENTS

Horn Studies

BRAHMS, JOHANNES (1833 - 1897)
____ (K09267) Ten Horn Studies, Op. posth

FRANZ, OSKAR (1843 - 1889)
____ (K04523) Etudes and Concert Etudes

KOPPRASCH, C.
____ (K04527) 60 Selected Studies

LEWY, JOS. RUDOLPH (1802 - 1881)
____ (K09268) Ten Progressive Etudes for Horn

Horn and Piano

BEETHOVEN, LUDWIG van (1770 - 1827)
____ (K09269) Horn Sonata, Op. 17
____ (K04521) Sonata in F Major, Op. 17 (for Horn and Piano)

HAAS, JOSEPH (1897 - 1960)
____ (K09270) Sonata in F

HAYDN, FRANZ JOSEPH (1732 - 1809)
____ (K04525) Horn Concerto No. 1 in D Major (Orch.)

MOZART, WOLFGANG AMADEUS (1756 - 1791)
____ (K04529) Concert-Rondo in E-flat Major, K. 371
____ (K03705) Horn Concerto No. 2 (E-flat Major, K. 417) (Orch.)
____ (K03709) Horn Concerto No. 3 (E-flat Major, K. 447) (Orch.)

HORN AND PIANO (Cont'd)

STRAUSS, RICHARD (1864-1949)
____ (K04130) Horn Concerto No. 1, Op. 11 (E-flat Major) (Orch.)

WEBER, CARL MARIA von (1786 - 1826)
____ (K04532) Concertino in E minor, Op. 45 (Orch.)

Two Horns

KLING, HENRI
____ (K04712) 30 Duets for Two Horns

NICOLAI, OTTO (1810 - 1849)
____ (K04715) Three Duets for Two Horns

Collection - Two Horns

DUETS FROM THE OLD MASTERS FOR TWO HORNS
____ (K04710) From Schubert, Telemann, Turraschmiedt and others

Collection - Three Horns

30 SELECTED WORKS FOR THREE HORNS
____ (K04842) Mozart, Mendelssohn, Kling, etc. (Parts)

Trumpet and Piano

BACH, JOHANN SEBASTIAN (1685 - 1750)
____ (K04538) Ten Preludes (Transcribed)

BALAY, GUILLAUME
____ (K04539) Piece de Concours

HAYDN, FRANZ JOSEPH (1732 - 1809)
____ (K04543) Trumpet Concerto (Orch.)

HUMMEL, JOHANN NEPOMUK (1778 - 1837)
____ (K04550) Trumpet Concerto

Trombone and Piano

GRAEFE, FRIEDEBALD
____ (K04558) Concerto

GUILMANT, ALEXANDER (1837 - 1911)
____ (K04559) Morceau Symphonique, Op. 88

JONGEN, JOSEPH (1873 - 1953)
____ (K09808) Aria and Polonaise, Op. 128

RIMSKY-KORSAKOV, NICOLAI (1844 - 1908)
____ (K04563) Trombone Concerto

WEBER, CARL MARIA von (1786 - 1826)
____ (K04566) Romance

Two Trombones

BLAZHEVICH, VLADISLAV
____ (K04708) Concert Duets for Two Trombones

Brass Quintet

HLOUSCHEK, THEODORE
____ (K09431) Three Pieces for Two Trumpets, Horn and Two Trombones

MIXED ENSEMBLES

Duos for Strings and Winds

BEETHOVEN, LUDWIG van (1770 - 1827)
___ (K04707)   Three Duets for Clarinet (B-flat) and Cello/Bassoon
___ (K04706)   Three Duets for Flute/Oboe/Violin and Cello/Bassoon

GLAZUNOV, ALEXANDER (1865 - 1936)
___ (K09763)   Ten Duets for Clarinet and Various Instruments

Trios for Flute, Violin and Cello (or Basso Continuo)

BACH, CARL PHILIPP EMANUEL (1714 - 1788)
___ (K04790)   Trio in B minor — P

HANDEL, GEORGE FRIDERIC (1685 - 1759)
___ (K04803)   Sonata in C minor, Op. 2, No. 1 — B.C. — P

TELEMANN, GEORG PHILLIP (1681 - 1767)
___ (K04825)   Suite No. 3 in B minor — B.C. — P
___ (K04826)   Suite No. 4 in E Major — B.C. — P

Trios for Two Flutes and Cello/Bass

BACH, WILHELM FRIEDEMANN (1710 - 1784)
___ (K04793)   Trio No. 1 in D Major for Two Flutes and Bass (Cello) — P

HAYDN, FRANZ JOSEPH (1732 - 1809)
___ (K03542)   Four London Trios

STAMITZ, CARL (1746 - 1801)
___ (K04820)   Trio in G Major

TELEMANN, GEORG PHILLIP (1681 - 1767)
___ (K04822)   Trio Sonata in C Major — P

Other Trios

BEETHOVEN, LUDWIG van (1770 - 1827)
___ (K03149)   Serenade, Op. 25 for Flute, Violin and Viola
___ (K04831)   Trio in C Major, Op. 87 for Two Oboes (or Violins) and English Horn

HANDEL, GEORGE FRIDERIC (1685 - 1759)
___ (K04002)   Trio No. 2 in D minor for Two Oboes and Bassoon (or Cello) — P

MOZART, WOLFGANG AMADEUS (1756 - 1791)
___ (K09691)   Trio in E-flat, K. 498 (Piano, Clarinet, Viola) — Sc.

TELEMANN, GEORG PHILLIP (1681 - 1767)
___ (K04823)   Trio Sonata in E minor for Flute, Oboe and B.C. — P

Quartets for Strings and Winds

MOZART, WOLFGANG AMADEUS (1756 - 1791)
___ (K09687)   Three Quartets, K. 285 (D Major) and K. 298 (A Major) — Violin, Viola, Cello and Flute; K. 370 (F Major) — Violin, Viola, Cello and Oboe

Other Ensembles for Strings and Winds

BACH, WILHELM FRIEDRICH ERNST (1759 - 1845)
___ (K09696)   Sextet in E-flat Major (Janetzky) (Violin, Viola, Cello, Clarinet and Two Horns)

BRAHMS, JOHANNES (1833 - 1897)
___ (K09673)   Clarinet Quintet, Op. 115 for Two Violins, Viola, Cello and Clarinet

DVORAK, ANTONIN (1841 - 1904)
___ (K03423)   Serenade, Op. 44 for Two Oboes, Two Clarinets in B-flat, Three Horns, Two Bassoons, Contra Bassoon (ad lib), Cello, Bass

HUMMEL, JOHANN NEPOMUK (1778 - 1837)
___ (K09943)   Septet, Op. 74 for Flute (or Oboe), Violin, Viola, French Horn, Cello, String Bass, and Piano

PROKOFIEV, SERGEI (1891 - 1953)
___ (K03806)   Overture on Hebrew Themes for Piano, Clarinet in B-flat and String Quartet (Op. 34)

SCHUBERT, FRANZ (1797 - 1828)
___ (K09460)   Octet in F Major, Op. 166 for String Quartet, String Bass, Clarinet, Horn and Bassoon

Other Ensembles for Winds and Brass

FIALA, JOSEPH (1748 - 1816)
___ (K09430)   Three Quintets for Two English Horns, Two Waldhorns and Bassoon

MOZART, WOLFGANG AMADEUS (1756 - 1791)
___ (K03733)   Divertimento No. 14 in B-flat Major, K. 270 for Two Oboes, Two Bassoons and Two Horns

Ensemble with Piano

SPOHR, LUDWIG (1784 - 1859)
___ (K09671)   Quintet in C minor, Op. 52 (Piano, Flute, Clarinet, Bassoon and Horn) — Sc.